I0166535

Remembrance

Remembrance

Madelyn Dunn

All rights reserved. No part of this publication may be reproduced, distributed, or transmitted in any form by any means, including photocopying, recording, or other electronic methods without the prior written permission of the author, except in the case of brief quotations embodied in reviews and certain other noncommercial uses permitted by copyright law. For permission requests, write to the author at the email address below.

madelyndunnpoetry@gmail.com

Copyright © 2025 Madelyn Jane Dunn
Printed in the United States of America
First Edition

ISBN 979-8-218-67646-9

First Printing, 2025

This book is dedicated to the people I've lost.
You taught me how to love
and how to live after that, too.

Contents

Dear Reader,

This book will wage a battle with your heart. It reflects on heartbreak and death, love and loss, forgiveness and remembrance.

These elements are key in the novel of life. Do they hurt? Yes. Are they worth experiencing to find out who you are? Another yes.

So, come along on this journey with me. Walk this slow, winding path through my life.

Let's explore the deepest corners of my heart and set my secrets free.

After all, who likes keeping them?

Madelyn.

Remembrance

Remembrance

Even though they say
time heals all wounds
the scars are still there
deep angry and red
carved into skin
like engravings on clay
my covering, porcelain
painted and cracked
pictures of flowers
filled with poison.

My soul splattered across the floor
pools of thoughts on the tiles
tomato red
blood spatters on my face
like hell's freckles
peppering me with a burning
a thick ache that spreads
from my wound to my chest
from my limbs to my head
and suddenly I can't seem to catch my—

breathe.
Just breathe.
That's all I hear.

Madelyn Dunn

I
 c
   a
     n
       ,
         t
          b
            r
             e
               a
                t
                  h
                    e

at the thought of you
my heart's still lying
beating slowly on the floor.

Rapids

Love is untouchable, unreachable.
It's not believable.
I stare at a figure in the clouds
and I hear melodic sounds
coming from it, like a song.
It makes me want to sing
but it's too far away to hear.
I reach towards it, holding back fear.

Love is untouchable, unreachable.
I'm stuck in this little bubble.
Love's a far away vision,
a chemical reaction.
I see it happen with others,
chemistry aligns and they smother
one another, creating a bond
with intertwined hands.

Love is untouchable, unreachable.
Sometimes I believe it isn't achievable,
Yet I see people living the dream.
Together, in love, floating down
love's river but I'm deathly afraid of rapids,
I figure they'll swallow me like acids
peel my skin apart layer by layer,
revealing my secrets.

Love is untouchable, unreachable.
It's pouring rain on a stormy day,
it's snow at the top of a mountain in winter,
it's predictable, yet so… beautiful.
It's the picture you wish you had painted.

Madelyn Dunn

Love is untouchable, unreachable.
It hasn't reached me yet. It's criminal
to make me wait this long for a crush.
I don't mind. I sit here and stare at the blush
of the sky, and my eyes drift
to someone sitting next to me, sitting adrift,
a boat in the river of love,
I climb into it and my heart soars.

Daisies

The future depends on the petals of a flower
the paper-like leaves of a daisy deciding
he loves me, he loves me not.

The pollen in the center, the runny yolk
of a bright ball of sun hanging in the sky.
If his feelings are like the center of this future-telling flower,
he loves me.

The stem of this daisy, picked long ago
withered and graying and falling apart
almost the shade of crying clouds.
If his feelings are like the dying stem of this flower,
he loves me not.

I think he loves a version of me
that I have spun
a piece that he has constructed in his mind
the easy version of me
the easy parts to love.

As I pick the final petal
my lips part to speak four little words:
he loves me not.

I should've known.
I should've known.
I should've known.

Madelyn Dunn

Dividing by Zero

My math teacher said to me:
"All arithmetic applies to real life."
I understand what he meant
putting things into numbers and symbols
can help explain even the toughest situation.

The irrational, never ending numbers
representing overthinking and anxiety
repeating and changing and flipping
and suddenly I'm just a decimal point
in a number to the billionth power.

The distribution property,
where one person can influence a group
multiply everything in the parentheses,
the restraints society places on us,
and you create a whole new monster
when negatives are added.

Did you know
you cannot divide by zero?
This is because
it has no multiplicative inverse
no number to times by to get the same
because when you give nothing
you get nothing.

A hundred times zero
still equals zero.
What if I gave 100 percent and you gave 0
and we still got together to make that nothing,

ending in "no solution."
What was the point
if all you were going to do
was divide by zero

rendering our time together useless
because who wants to remember
the irrational numbers and decimal points
that make up my shattered heart?

Madelyn Dunn

Thirteen

There are thirteen lines within this poem,
thirteen opportunities to tell you
all about my good luck
that most people would consider bad.

I vividly remember breaking a mirror
while I was studying at thirteen years old,
shattered remains glistening around me.
I walk under ladders, adopt black cats,
I wish that every time I get a race bib,
It's thirteen.

Bad luck for others is good luck for me
tragedy turns to ecstasy
and isn't that always good to see?

Underground

Deep underground there lies
a million people
lost to disease
famine
old age

simple stones to commemorate their lives
some have temples dedicated in their honor
many have been lost to time

I wish I could remember them all.

How does one remember the forgotten?
How does one find the lost?
How does one live after a death?

How can I move on when
I feel their memory slipping already
mere moments after I lost them?

I only have one fear
the fear that I will lose them
to the chaos of my mind.

Madelyn Dunn

Open Wound

My heart beats loudly in my ears
the blood rushing to it to calm my fears
when it reaches, it pours out of my chest
my senses heightening to a crest
I feel the warm sensation drip down my skin
and it feels like something I might win.

The feeling intensifies as I breathe
and I hear a blade slide into its sheath
the burning spread
washing over me and engulfing my head.
I'm overcome with a sense of doubt
that I'm going to make it out.

I claw at the person from behind,
silently wondering, do I have a mind?
A thought large enough to protect,
thinking about it, and I connect
a small light, flickering in the dark
I guide myself towards that mark.

I see light at the end of that tunnel
my thoughts turn towards that funnel
the injury scarred into a thin line
every time I'm asked about it, I say I'm fine
but you stabbed me with your words,
dug into me with talons, like a bird's.

You drew your knife out just to attack again,
pulling at my insides, like a bad physician
I was lost in a red sea of my own

floating in agony all alone.
My heart almost bled out
yet I crawled past you and found my doubts
threw them away and clawed at the ground
traveling in pain until—
I found a way to escape this open wound.

Madelyn Dunn

Painting the Sky

Death is a strange thing,
it hides behind flowers and candies
peeks out from bushes and trees
following everyone until it's their time.

His time came too soon,
too fast, taken from us too early.
Death wrapped its hands around him
like a light breeze on his shoulders
I like to think he went peacefully
softly falling asleep
only to never wake up again.

The way he shaped my life
with his hands, his words, his spirit
it was ripped away in an instant

but he made a promise to me before he left
an unspoken agreement, a quiet whisper
we'd watch the sunsets together
and he'd murmur
something about paint and the sky.

I never understood until now
as I sit atop a hill and stare out at the ombre
the orange fading to pink and gold
he was painting the sky

he was making it beautiful,
just for me.

Twist the Knife

I'm still heartbroken over you,
no matter the trials you put me through.
How did I go so wrong?
Losing you was like getting stabbed
my heart practically gave out.
It took months for it to finally come back
to reality, the wound slowly closing.
It's all a blur.

I was so, so close to healing
I could almost touch that feeling
then, I saw you and her.
My stomach flipped, I felt panic occur.
You took her to *our* place.
My brain took off into space.

My body froze from the chill
it took everything in me not to spill
to let my emotions take over my mind
my vision glazed over and I felt blind.
I was so, so close to healing.
The feeling I felt was so revealing.
Seeing you caused me deep sorrow—
And then you twisted the knife.

My heart started openly bleeding,
I begged on my knees, pleading
to anyone for a glimmer of help
a light in the dark, I let out a yelp
the pain spread like a dull ache
I laid there until daybreak,

Madelyn Dunn

warm sun splashed over my injuries,
healing them like a balm.
My body is a storm, my blood is the rain.
It's just too much, I cry out in pain.
You twisted the knife you embedded in me.
That was something I could never foresee.

Us.

Where did we go wrong?
I thought we were forever,
our time with one another would go on
years and years, always together.

I haven't texted you in a year.
I haven't heard your voice
because of hope and fear.
I'm afraid I'll have to make a choice.

A choice about us.
Where did we go wrong?
Maybe on the bus,
we sat too close, listened to a song.
The lyrics changed and I looked at you
I felt a feeling stir inside
I no longer felt blue.
Would I be yours?

I thought I was your favorite.
Around you, I felt divine.
You gave me that bracelet
It spelled out, "Mine."
I never took it off.
It frayed and wore down
People would scoff,
"It's worthless," and frown.

It meant everything to me.
A symbol of our unbreakable bond.
How was it so fragile, the idea of us?

Madelyn Dunn

I never thought something would be beyond
us, like we would have lasted
through summer storms and winter snow.
Oh, how my dreams and reality contrasted.

The numbness consumed me when you left.
My eyes wept, I would have a fresh start.

You and me, us and we,
we're not friends or enemies,
just strangers with memories.

Clouds

Salty tears run down
my face. Clouds, pouring out rain
are crying with me.

Madelyn Dunn

Ghosted

I've been ghosted
and it hurts
to be left on delivered for weeks
to be sent pictures of the ceiling
because I "don't deserve to see your face"
to be told by your friends
that you don't like me anymore,
but I still like you.

Did you know that?
I still want you.
but it's fine that you don't.
Perfectly fine
because I'm used to being second place
but know this feeling won't last an eternity.

Facing Death

I believe
that I have stared
death in the face.

I was diagnosed with Lyme disease
caught right as it became severe.
In my dreams,
the night before the swelling occurred
I dreamt I was facing death
just a black shadow with a ghostly smile.

I stared at him
not sure what to say
and a laugh bubbled in my throat,
spilling out like rapids in a river.

I laughed in the face of death,
maybe that's why I survived.

Madelyn Dunn

Why?

Sometimes I wish he never left.
Sometimes I wish he came back.
Sometimes I wish he loved me.
Sometimes I wish he never tried.

Because who could love
an already defective heart?
You'd think it would be untouched
since nothing romantic had interacted with it
yet it was broken
a million times over
and he couldn't fix it.

That was
the worst day
of my life,

when seashells tickled my legs
and sunshine reigned over our
sandy kingdom,

when he told me he loved me,
and I just asked why.

Called It Rain

Falling in love is like setting the world on fire.
You light the match and it ignites, expanding,
it never stops growing and changing,
destroying everything in its path.
Those obstacles have nothing on us

until the world is on fire
and we're surrounded.
Everyone is gone
and this is our fault.
We set this world on fire and called it rain
and now, we're the ones burning up.

As the flames lick my calves,
I look at my lover one last time
his face tells me the whole story.
He didn't want to set this world on fire,
at least, not with me.

Madelyn Dunn

How Long Will It Hurt?

How long will the thought of you
cause my heart to spasm and stutter?

How long will the pictures of you
make me cry uncontrollably?

How long will my lips stay dry
because I can't bear to touch
where you once kissed?

How long will losing you
losing *us*
ruin me?

Because I can't take anymore.
How long will it hurt?

So Many Signs

I didn't love you
no matter how hard I tried.
Why, why, why
did the world curse me like this?
Making me lose the only love I ever had?
Because I was scared.

I couldn't stand looking at him
feeling his eyes on mine
I thought I was in love
maybe it would've been divine.
My soul was crushed by him,
and I don't know why.

His only crime
was loving me too much
and I left
because I couldn't do it.

Too intense.
Too fast.
It was all too much…

and God, I didn't want to break his heart
but mine was already gone.

Madelyn Dunn

Between Stars

Losing someone
feels like a part of your heart
has rotted and fallen out,
a hollowed shell lying there.

Even though I know
his soul is between the stars
up in the sky,
making constellations shine
I can't help
but miss him.

How do you go on
when the person who you loved so much
is completely removed from your life?

How do you survive
knowing they aren't with you anymore?

How can you act normally
when it hits you that they're gone?

My heart is a graveyard of memories
moments of my time with him.
I will treasure those snippets
until I join him in the afterlife.

For now, he will reside
in a little pocket in my heart
between the stars of remembrance
and the reminders of loss.

Broken

The broken sobs that spilled
from my body
made him shiver
begging to run into my arms
but he couldn't
and he never would
because that would prove I won
and the only thing I know anymore
is that he would never, ever let me win.

Stolen Innocence

You felt
so loved, yet so alone.
Were you naïve?
No.
God, of course not.

You didn't know better,
nobody could.
In your eyes
he was a sweet guy
a boy who *loved* you.

Did he really?
You can answer that question yourself.
If he had the capability
to treat such a wonderful woman like you
like that.
He never deserved you in the first place.

He stole your innocence
stole your soft, angel-winged heart
and broke it into a million pieces.

Neglected

Treasured in secret
but ignored in the light.

Why did he
love you in the dark
but not when
the spotlight shifted onto you?

In private, he was a lover
yet in public, he was a stranger.

You didn't exist around his friends
why were you okay with that?

Because being neglected in the moment
was better than never being loved.

Silent love was better than nothing,
right?

Madelyn Dunn

Despondency

"Homecoming is supposed to be
the best night of your freshman year,"
everyone said.

You felt ecstatic
he took pictures with you,
and you felt so, so pretty
you thought, "finally, I'm happy."

Flickering disco lights and
booming music that
drummed in your ears
like an earthquake.

Dancing like no one was watching
until he disappeared,
where was he?

Oh.
He was dancing with another girl.
Another girl.
Someone who wasn't you.

Your heart
was dragged into a pit of despair
you clawed at the edge,
holding on for dear life

but you couldn't stay there.
Your hand slipped
you tumbled into the abyss
heartbreak enveloping your lungs.

Your friends tried to calm you down
held you as you sobbed
as if a sponge could hold back a flood.

They couldn't do anything
to stop this wave of despondency
they couldn't stop it
from drowning you.

Madelyn Dunn

Light Them Up

Picture this:

You are a candle
lit on fire
beautiful flames dancing on your body
melting you eternally.

Your friend has a tough time
lighting her own candle,
you would help her
right?

Because a candle doesn't lose anything
by lighting another…

and yet, you still hurt others.
Calling them names
is like blowing out their candle.

Light them up. Don't blow them out.

Candles

You'd do anything to make him feel
the same pain you felt when he cheated.

You'd do just about anything
to make his heart crack and splinter
shattering into an impossible puzzle

but at the same time
you wish he still loved you.
You still love him,
even after what he did.

Take your revenge and
find another flame,
one who brightens your heart
better than he ever did.

Avenge the lost love
by realizing it was never sincere.

Let that fire engulf him.
Let it burn him up.

Madelyn Dunn

Half-love

I wanted you to love me
only wanted you to truly care
to feel your hand as you take the key
to my heart, you run a hand through my hair
kiss me on my forehead
a soft puff of cold air.
Too bad your feelings for me are dead.
It's like an inequality expression, not fair.

One half is greater than the other
my love > your reciprocated love.
I couldn't seem to smother
the burning fire writhing in and above.

Heart wrapped in chains of godforsaken fire
branding me with scars of our time together
and the echoing sounds of a choir
covered the marks with sleeves of leather.

Hide the scars, hide the remains.
Hide the forgetful flames.
Hide all that you lost and won.
Hide the slashes of a half-loved run.

He Wasn't Mine

My heart broke before we were over.
I knew he wasn't my four-leaf clover
I think— no, I know— he felt it too
we came apart like our glue
had failed us, desperately clung together
I figured we'd break apart in September
at the end of summer and peacefully part.
I knew we'd grow apart
but I didn't think it would hurt this terribly
and my heart burns unbearably.

I'm in your backpack, looking for sunscreen
I see something that makes me turn green
I drop the backpack and hold it in my hand
a circlet of metal, a bracelet or band
I cover my mouth as I recognize
It's hers and I cry out in surprise.
Why does he have her jewelry?
I heave it into the cruel sea.

I cried for hours before I told him,
didn't want to say it on a whim
I waited until they were both there
and waited until I didn't care
finally confronted them, emotionlessly
they sat there as I talked hopelessly
they admitted to hanging out and
I stand.
That's when I realized—
he was never mine,
just someone I'd idealized.

Madelyn Dunn

Kissing

Kiss me until I'm sick from the taste of your lips.

My mouth was swollen and when I touched it,
it felt like you blessed me.
An angel's soft, delicate lips on mine
my stomach hurt when you left.
I longed for your touch.

Your lips were inflamed,
they were pink and pillowy and so soft.
I wish I could bottle the feeling I got
when I looked at my handiwork:
you let me do that to you
you let me kiss you.

Now, I can't kiss you anymore,
but I still feel sick.

Numb

~~My heart beats for you~~
My heart used to beat for you
of course, you knew that.

Now it only beats for blood.
~~My soul still longs for you~~
My soul used to yearn for you

but now I can't feel anything at all.
Why can't I love again?
~~Because you ruined me~~

Because you loved me too hard, too fast.
That's why I had to leave.
It was too much. It was overwhelming.

But I cannot feel anymore—
none of the palpitations against my chest,
since now you're gone.

You took with you
a love I couldn't stand.
Did he know the real me?
~~Of course he didn't.~~

Did he even love me? ~~God, I hope so.~~
Will I ever experience love again?
~~No. I'm numb.~~

Madelyn Dunn

Empty Hands

I begged on my knees for you to stay.
I held out my hands for a single drop of
your love, your blood, your heart.
I was left there, my palms facing upward,
waiting to be filled.
They never would be.

I begged on my knees for you to stay.
You had to go away.
I didn't have it in myself to go with you.
I wish I had.
You knew I wasn't strong enough to leave,
and you pried your hands from mine and ran.

I begged on my knees for you to stay.
Every ounce of my body longed for you,
but here we are, separated again.
I wanted you forever, you know.
I thought we were endgame.

I begged on my knees for you to stay.
And now I wait here, my hands still outstretched,
waiting for you to choose me.
I still sit here, with empty hands,
reminiscing on the times
when I thought you would fill them.

"Time Heals All Wounds"

That is just a lie
people tell you
when their cuts
are only splinters.
A real, deep wound
will never fully close.
It throbs with the heartbeat
of your lost lover.

Madelyn Dunn

Her Name on Your Lips

You used to whisper the letters
making up the sounds of my name
every syllable wrapping me in sandpaper.

God, I was sick of it.
Your words filling me with poison,
and my teeth I would grit.
It took all I had to stop my eyes moistening
you filled my heart with false lies
soft, pretty words, yet they broke my soul.
I thought you would be my prize
never knew that high of a toll
could be taken on my shattered heart.

Because her name was on your lips too,
all the time, every day.

How could a girl so in love be so blue?
How did he lead her so far astray?
How did she know her heart would break?
How could she stand that wait?
How could she feel that embedded stake?

I knew my name wasn't the only one.
Her name, on your lips.
Same lips, pressed against mine, would stun
my heart, shatter it in two. My stomach flips.
The lips with which you speak her name,
are kissing mine, the very same.

Fresh

Those words hit me hard
you told me you didn't love me
after I bared my heart and soul to you
and even though I hate it
I still love you
with every bone in my body.
You don't know how much you affect me.

I lie in bed and think of you
over and over and over until I'm sobbing.
If I could got another chance
to love someone else,
I hate to say this,
but I'd still choose you.

You may think it's scabbed over,
that I'm over you,
that I love someone else,
that I finally found "the one,"
but it's still fresh.

Madelyn Dunn

Duct Tape

"How to fix a broken heart"
I begin to type.
I backspace and rewrite,
"How to fix a slightly cracked heart"
That's what it is, really.

Slightly broken.
Just a little mangled.
Only a few heartstrings snapped.
It's nothing, compared to others' pain.
It was real to me, though.

"Duct tape should fix it."
I cut a little slice off the end of the roll
and tape the wound shut.
It slides right off the soaked wound.
Pumping with blood,
so much I almost faint from the loss of it.

If duct tape can't fix my broken heart,
what can?

Happy Ever After

It doesn't come as easy
as it seems.
The glass slippers cut your feet,
pumpkins don't make very good carriages, either
and, of course, the one stipulation,
it all returns to normal at midnight.

Along with
the one person
I wanted to spend my life with,
gone at the strike of twelve.
A hole in my heart
where he once resided.

He left
not by choice,
by magical law,
but I get the feeling
he didn't even want to stay.

Madelyn Dunn

Something Tells Me

Something tells me I wasn't the only one
not the only name his lips spoke
because the way he was holding me
it's like he held someone else too
who taught him the ways to love
but I don't want a half-used heart.

Something tells me I could've been better:
better to him, to his friends, to mine.
When could I ever be good enough?
Did I have to sacrifice myself to hide
not loving the boy who loved me?

Something tells me I could've loved him
if we had known each other longer.
It was a rushed relationship
a summer fling that ended quickly.
In another universe,
would I love him, if I'd have had the time?

Something tells me I wouldn't want to know
what could possibly happen between us
because what if he leaves again?

Could I love him?
Something tells me I wouldn't even try.

After the Party

There's cake all over the floor
we smashed it there long before
spilled drinks on the couch
and all over my brand-new dress
I said I didn't mind
but God, I did.

I wanted to look pretty
for him, understandably
I felt amazing as he saw me
called me beautiful.
We danced until the sun rose:
a promise of a new love.

A Shirley Temple
splashed on my white dress
I felt the color of the grenadine
spread to my cheeks
the blush on my face matching the stain
my mascara sliding onto my under-eyes
mixing with the drops of liquid despair.

I ran away from
my biggest fear.

I ran and I ran and I ran until
I couldn't run anymore
and I was lost
all alone in the sea
of embarrassment.

Madelyn Dunn

What did I find there
but the version of myself
I thought I'd lost all those years ago.

In the midst of the afterparty
I found myself
because of a stain
on my beautiful white dress.

Shower Thoughts

Why did you
think it was funny
to play with my feelings
to tell me you loved me
and then leave?

Why couldn't you
wait until I was ready?
Why did you have to
push ahead, like fire
leaving me in the embers?

I didn't love you
I think we both knew that
so why did I cry when you left?

Why do I want to text you
and tell you all these things
when I know I can't?

Because shower thoughts
are supposed to stay quiet.

Madelyn Dunn

~~Lunatics~~ *Lovers*

~~They call me a lunatic~~
I am purely a *lover*
I'm just a ~~lunatic~~ *little girl* in love
so far gone
~~I dove into the pit of insanity~~
I dove into the pit of *veneration*.
You came with me.

They call us ~~lunatics~~ *full of passion*
~~we're insane.~~
We're just *in love*
right?
~~We're insane~~
we love each other
we're perfectly sane.

…right?

…right?

My Name

My name spells out the truths of my life
just through a few letters and syllables.

M aybe I'm just naïve
A nd he wasn't trying to break me
D o I really believe that?
E specially after his confession that he
L oved me right before he left
Y ou and I both know he
N ever meant it.

Madelyn Dunn

Lost His Mind

He tried to understand every
thought inside my head
with a single question:

"Are you okay?"

How does one tell
the person who loves them the most
that they feel lost and unwanted
and alone in this world?

He begged for me to let him in
"I'm here for you" he claimed.

Little did he know
he would lose his mind
trying to understand mine.

Missing What I Never Had

Lately
I've been missing.
Missing you.
Missing our love,

but I never
never, never, never
loved you.

I'd rather count
the sands in an hourglass
watching my own time tick away
than choose
between you and myself.

You say you loved me,
but not in the past, present or future,
will I believe that
a girl like me
was adored by you?

I am an acquired taste
yet you chose me.

How am I missing something I never had?

Madelyn Dunn

Diagnosis

What would have happened
if I had not woken up that morning
aching in pain?
What would have happened?

Would I have lived to see
another birthday,
wedding,
final exam,
party,
or fireworks on the fourth of July?

Would I be able to laugh
at the smudged lead on the side of my hand
in the middle of the teacher's lecture?

Would I be where I am now,
writing a poem in my bedroom,
on a Sunday in September?

I would not be here today
if it weren't for
a swollen knee.

Thank you
to my body
for saving me.

Treasure

When most people think of treasure
they think of a pirate's chest
precious gold and jewelry spilling out of it
but when I think of treasure
I think of writing.

The only one who would take care of me
who would forgive me when I'm mean
who would love me through thick and thin.

I always wondered if perfection exists
and now I know it does.

Most hobbies are only built on expression,
but writing, the art of telling a story,
it builds an escape hatch
and yanks you through the door.

Madelyn Dunn

Our Own World

Can we create our own world?
Where every word we speak is reality?
Where we can have as much fun as we want?
Where we can love each other with no repercussions?
Where we can feel good about ourselves?
Where we can feel no pain?

Scratch that last one
I already feel no pain when I'm with you.
The overwhelming sense of love
it feels so right yet so wrong at the same time.
Maybe I could learn to love you without holding back.
Maybe I could learn to forget the others and only think of you.
Maybe we're already in our own world.

Sun Shower

The way love makes you feel is like a sun shower.
When the rain is drizzling down,
but you stand in the
bright rays of sun
that shine on your face like angels' kisses
warm rain decorates your skin in rainbows
you spin and twirl under the sensations of it all.

You dance until your legs hurt.
And when you sit down on the ground afterwards
you have the biggest smile on your face
that would make anyone on this Earth
feel like they're over the moon.

Madelyn Dunn

Always On My Mind

Why are you always on my mind?
I'll be thinking and suddenly find
an image of you within my thoughts.
My brain is taken over like it was bought
and everyday I hope and pray
that you'd think about me the same way.

Why am I always thinking about you?
I can't focus on something as simple as two plus two
when you're around. My mind goes blank
as if it's the edge of a riverbank
the dirt gets washed away by the stream
I never wanted to constantly scream
in joy, I told my friends about you, and they laughed.
I obsess over everything I love about you,
even if you only love me half as much as I love you.

It's okay, because I forgive and forget
I remember and I regret
but most of all, I stay true:
me, wishing for you.
and you, hoping for me too.

It Was Always You

It was always you
we both knew it.
I only ever wanted one person:
you.
I wanted you.

I wanted all of you.
Your good days
and the bad too.

I would've torn myself apart
just to see a smile
dance on your lips,
like a ghost.

I never wanted anything except you
but at the same time
each one of these things I did
unreciprocated
I was told that's how love works.

And now I've made the verdict
that I never loved you
I was tearing myself apart.

Love comes from within
but what did I have left to give?

Madelyn Dunn

Infected

You've got an incurable disease
something that'll plague your mind
for the rest of your days.

You've got that feeling
that it's going to stick with you forever
whether you embrace it or break it.

You know you won't forget this one
not now, not ever
it's too special, too fragile, too… perfect.

You and him, right?
It's always been you two
against the world.

Now you're stuck in the quarantine zone
you've both been infected with the deadliest disease of all:
falling in love.

Almost

I miss you
I know I chose this
to let it trail off, I suppose
but I miss you so much.

I miss when you were amazed by me
It's not too much to ask to have someone
voice their happiness for you, is it?

I loved it when you told me I was amazing
special, wonderful, perfect.
We were so happy.

And I wish I was still on your mind
would you still be proud of me?
That's why I almost texted you.

Madelyn Dunn

I Think I Love You

I think I love you
I couldn't see it until now
just in time for me to lose you

I think I love you

I see it in the sunsets
the blizzards
hurricanes
thunderstorms
I see you everywhere

Now, I could shout
"I love you"
and you're too far across the world
to hear it.

Chaos

We were a raging storm:
kisses and thunder
lightning and love letters.

My beloved, the rain.
I was in the sky.
He fell from me, like an angel.

Soft blond hair and sky-blue eyes
I imagine him with feathery white wings.
Did he come from heaven?

If he was Eros, I was Psyche
given impossible tasks yet accomplished
I would've jumped off a cliff for him.

They say chaos is all claws and snarls
but they never warn you
that chaos can come in the form of
innocent first loves.

Madelyn Dunn

Messages to the Moon

When night becomes
synonymous with loss,
one begins to send
messages to the moon.

"Please come back.
The sky is so dark without you."

Then moon peeks out
from behind the dark clouds
and responds,
"You have to light the way for yourself."

Salty tears fell from
her dark eyes
as she stared
quietly at him.

One could tell
by glancing at her gaze,
that she was gone forever.

All she wrote to him was,
"I need you."

Surrender

I swore I wouldn't surrender
that I wouldn't fall in love
but now I'm breaking that promise.
I love him so dearly
so much that I have to.
They cannot make me
want to not love him.
It's not physically possible.

Madelyn Dunn

Infinity

Our love is like
trying to paint the sky.
There is no way you can
capture the beauty.
The feeling of there
being so much of it.

Our love is like
trying to count stars.
There is no way you can
count every one.
The feeling of being
a little speck in the world.

Our love is like
trying to count the
never-ending digits of pi.

All of these things are
endless, forever.

Our love is infinity. ∞

Backseat Driver

My life isn't mine
I'm the driver yet I don't decide where to go:
people in the back
bombarding me with directions
I can't make one decision without their reactions changing my mind.
Shrill voices echo in my ears.
Traffic lights blaring at me through the windshield.

Why should I listen to them?
Why should I deal with their backseat driving?
I swerved the wheel and took control.

Madelyn Dunn

Clockwork

My life is like a clock.
It goes around in heavenly circles
and always returns to the old ways.
The hands move slowly,
yet always keep moving.

Sometimes, I break down.
I have to be wound up again
but when I get back
I'm stronger than ever.

It's quite easy to break a clock
but it's nearly impossible to fix.

Be careful with this clock of mine
because it's really just my heart
so truly divine.

Slow Growth

You're always growing
always changing for the better.

But while I wait,
each breath feels like lead on my lips
occupying my mind at every waking moment.

I remember when I started writing
poems took a while.
Now, the words just bloom from my thoughts.
People say practice makes perfect
but perfect isn't possible.
There's always room for growth
slow, slow growth.

Madelyn Dunn

Locked in a Jar

I awake surrounded by walls
the material that breaks when it falls.
Slide against the glass and feel
like a fish in a sink
inevitably waiting for the drain to swallow
me whole, and my life would follow
and I'd be taken adrift by the water
getting spun like clay on a potter's wheel.
The water fills my lungs and—

I sharply inhale and my brain goes on a spiel.
It's not real.
I'm still in this glass jar feeling the appeal
of being the fish in the bowl.
I'd rather be burnt up by coal
than sit here for another second
and suddenly I'm a tired deckhand
sitting on the upper floor of a boat.
I stand up and dive into the water. I float
and I think about being free,
as free as one can be
when locked in a jar.

I wish for any sense of hope. It's too far.

One Frosty Morning

You have to be strong to rise with the sun
rising earlier and earlier each day
the sun nourishes all
but what happens when the sun goes dark?

When it's thunder, lightning, rain
all around you
you're in the eye of the hurricane
and all you can see is the destruction raging through

the sun morphing into a pearly moon
glistening in the sky, almost blazing.
The flowers crust with ice
frosting over and wilting
your breath becomes glazed in front of you.

The world freezes over and
all the humans in the world
have one thing in common:
frozen hearts beating anew.

Madelyn Dunn

Perfectionism

I'm tearing myself apart
because I can't be perfect
but I need to be.

I am melting between icicles and morning dew,
falling into the graves I dug,
lying in this imperfect bed I created.

The house of cards is falling down
my spine is cracking into a thousand pieces
birds stop singing, plants stop growing
everything snaps into
fragments of loss.

Perfectionism (Redone)

Watch me
as I scrawl my signature on the table
but erase it every time.
Why?

Because it wasn't good enough.
The M was too big,
the y too small,
my name disgracing me as I write it
over and over,
cursing my shaky hands.

My hands tremble when I think of failing
but "failure is part of life" they say
I guess my life won't be complete.

But to prove something to myself,
I left my name on the table
even if it wasn't as perfect as I wished.

Madelyn Dunn

Never Again

I once trusted someone so much
that I told her my darkest secret.
I thought she would never let it go.
I trusted her to keep silent.

I thought she would listen to me
telling her to never, ever tell anyone.
I trusted her to keep that whisper close
in a tight hug, inescapable.
When I wasn't looking, she tossed it onstage.
It seemed as if every light in the world focused on it
and the worst part?
I knew she was going to do that.

Second chances are dumb.
If someone hurts you once,
it'll happen again and again and again.
You give them chance after chance,
thinking they'll learn.

They will never change
they know what they're doing
and they don't care.

Jigsaw

Chest pains
wracking my entire body in spasms
I was losing him, my mind knew it.
My heart wouldn't accept half of it was gone
splitting right down the middle.

I didn't want to leave,
to lose the last piece in the puzzle.
Scratch that, he was the picture it made up.
Is there any way to learn
how to piece something back together without a guide?

Someone dug those pieces out
put them back together
but the damage had already been done
my heart already cut to smithereens
the jigsaw leaving jagged marks on it
the blood beating quicker and quicker as
betrayal carved her initials into my heart.
Those marks would be there forever.

Madelyn Dunn

Mágoa

Have you ever been in love?
It's a wonderful, dazzling, blinding feeling
it makes you feel like you're dancing in the rain,
smiling up at the crying clouds.
It makes you whole again

until it's ripped away from you
taking all of the effort you poured into it.
Why did I love someone who wasn't forever?

Mágoa is a love so real, so passionate
it leaves scars on your heart when it's gone
those marks are there forever
maybe they'll scab over
maybe they'll fade
but there will always be a little white line
a little scratch that makes you alive.

It proves to you that you are capable of love
and that you're worthy of healing.

My Cave

Have you ever read Plato's allegory?

Three humans are chained in a cave since birth
they face the wall and experience life
by watching the shadows dance across it
they never know anything else besides them.

One day, a prisoner breaks free
and visits the outside world
he sees love for the first time
he experiences heartbreak and death
he comes back to his friends
and tells them about the wonders he saw
the horrors too.

They don't believe him.
How could the shadows,
the only things they'd ever known, just be reflections?
They refused his explanation.
The end of that story isn't important, not in my eyes.

As humans, we're all in our own cave
we will not escape, like that man did
instead, we expand our cave
build tunnels to connect with our loved ones.

I built a path to your cave
then watched you seal your side shut
the tunnel collapsed in on itself
when you let the ceiling of it drop;
it ruined mine, too.

Madelyn Dunn

You left your mark in my cave
cracks from the gaping, earth-filled hole
splintering on the ceiling like spiderwebs.

I tried to dig it out again
to no avail
yet I tried every day.
But just as I was about to break through,
I gave up

because if you let it collapse
then I might as well not build it up again.

Acknowledgments

This book would not have been possible without the unwavering support from so many people in my life.

To my closest friend—Alexandria—thank you for your encouragement and laughter. Every time I messaged you late at night, asking for a read-through of a poem or simply to talk, you were there.

A special thank you to Mr. Charles Renz, whose passion for the written word has shaped me in ways I can never fully express. Your belief in me has meant more than you know.

To my mother and father—thank you for your endless love of me and my dreams. Your support has built the foundation upon which I stand today.

To everyone I have loved and lost along the way, thank you for teaching me lessons I could never have learned on my own. Even though I no longer walk beside you, you will always reside in my heart.

With immense gratitude and appreciation,

Madelyn

About the Author

Madelyn Dunn is a student, part-time poet, and aspiring journalist who lives in the suburbs of Philadelphia. When she's not writing, you can find her thumbing through the latest edition of the New York Times, debating political issues in Model UN, and reading dystopian literature. Her poetry often explores themes of loss, love, and the lengths people will go to for both. You can find her at @madelyndunnwriting on Instagram.

www.ingramcontent.com/pod-product-compliance
Lightning Source LLC
LaVergne TN
LVHW051755080426
835511LV00018B/3326